Frogs and Sea Turtles Adults Coloring Book

This Coloring book belongs to:

____

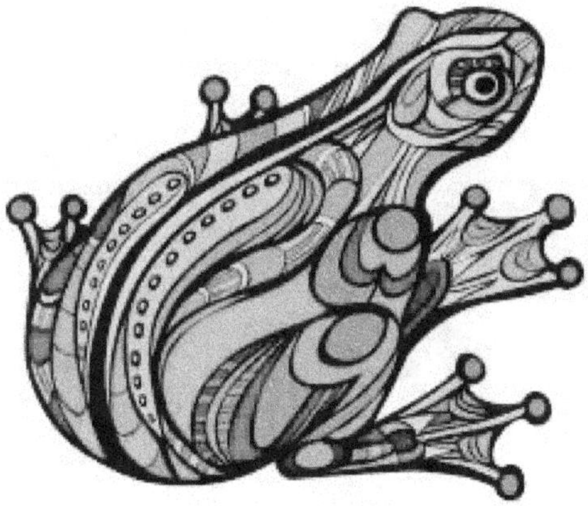

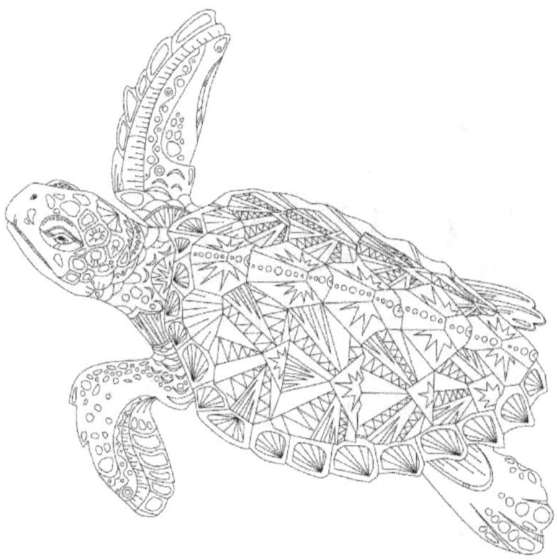

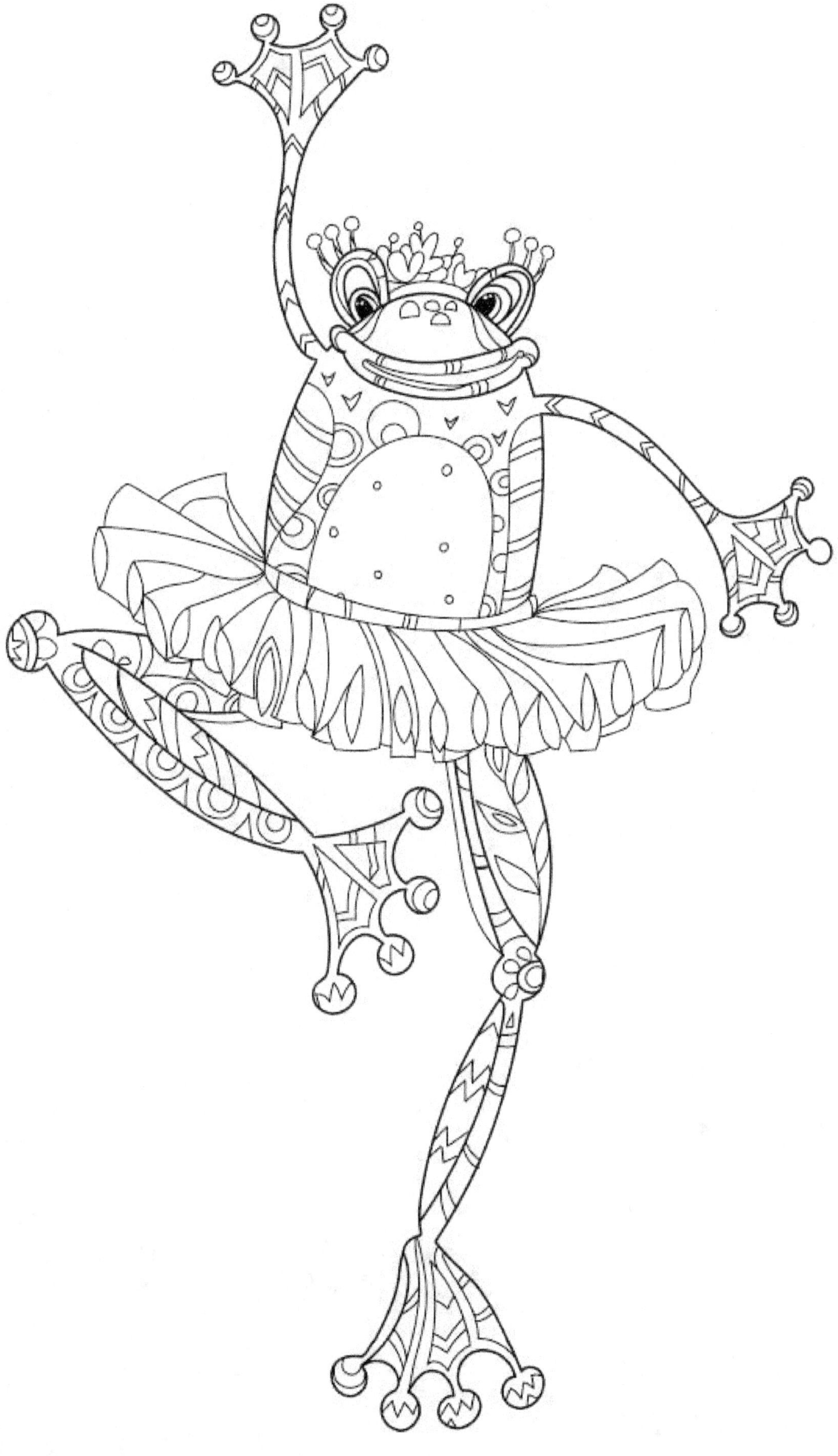

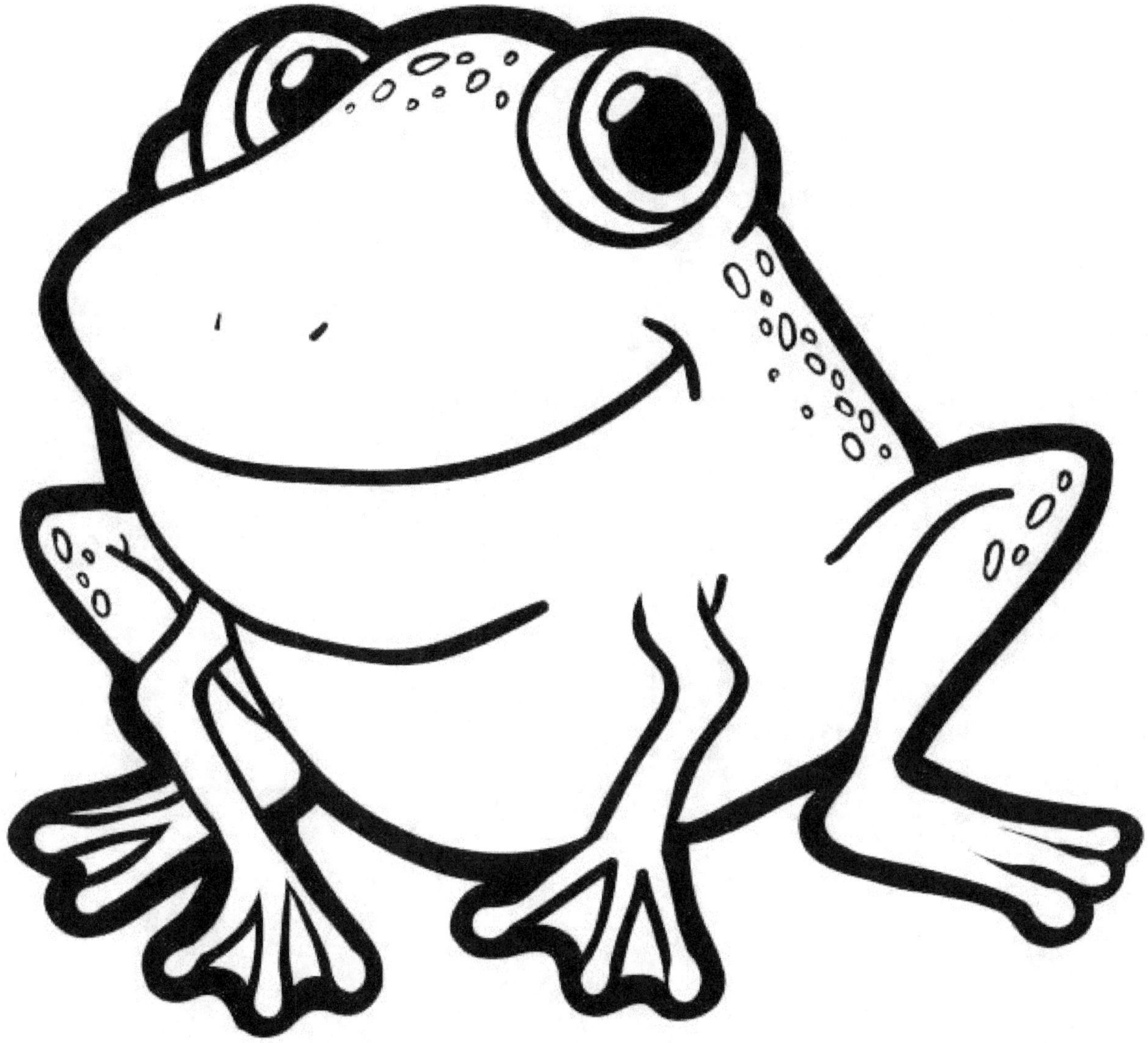

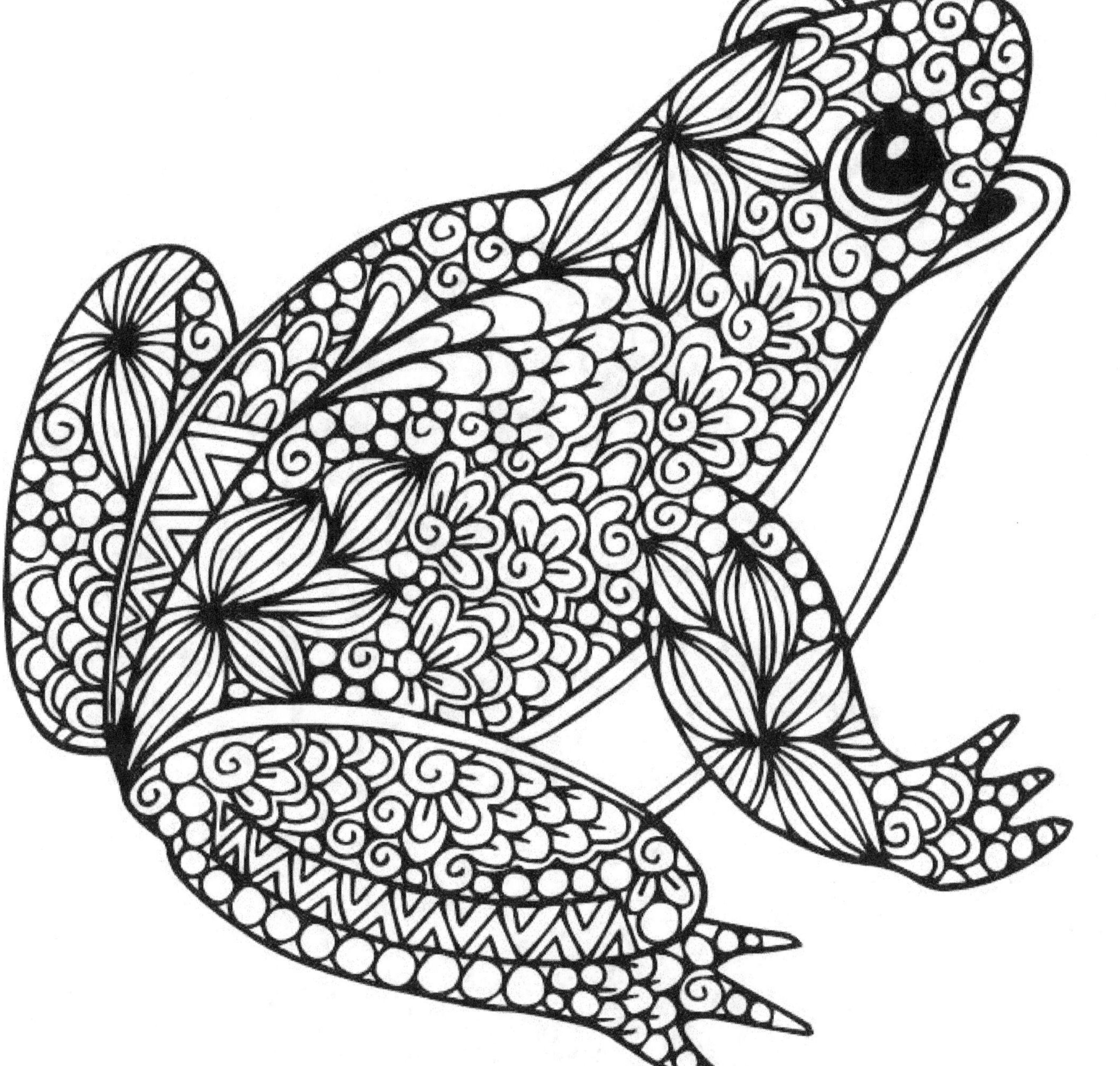

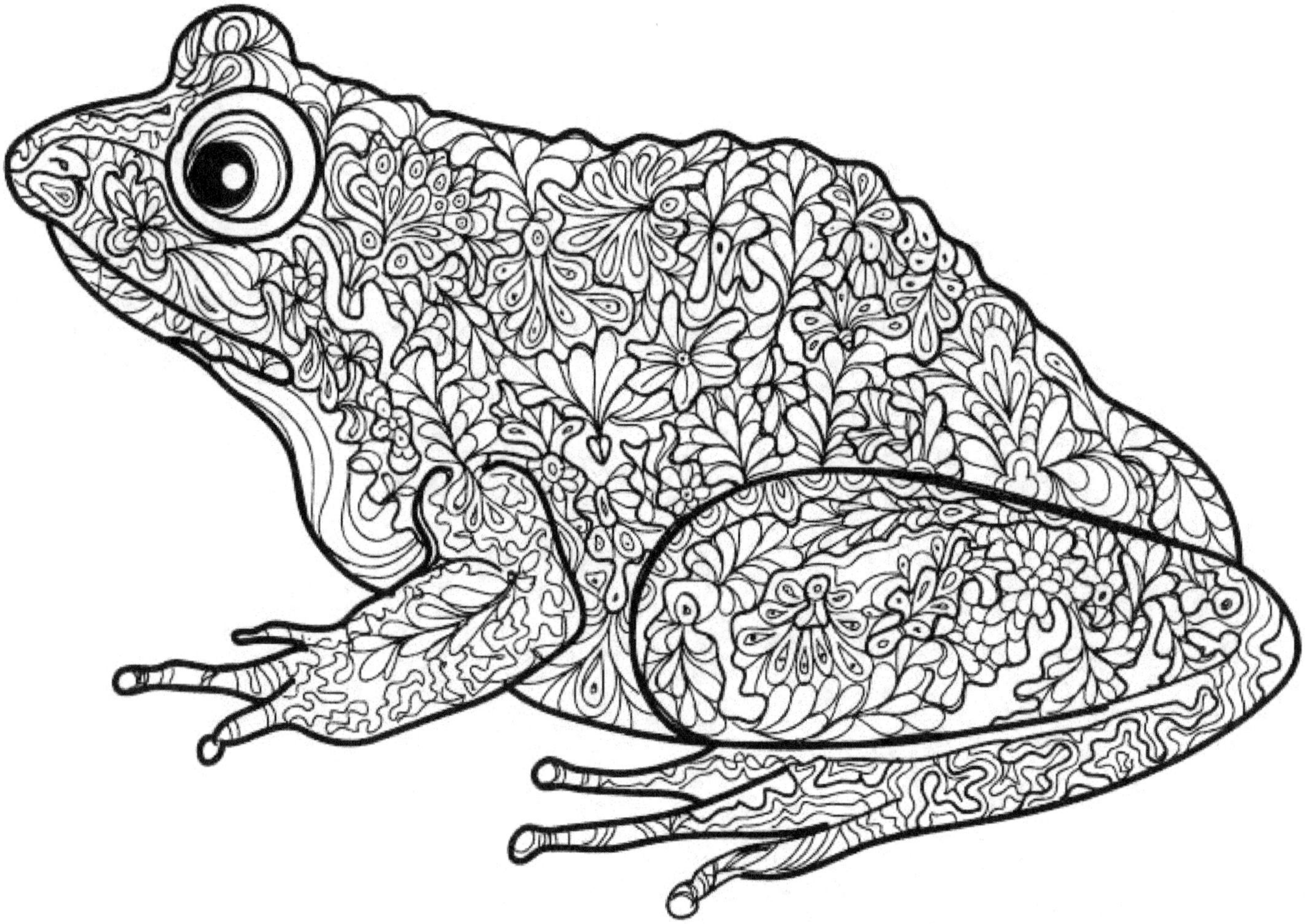

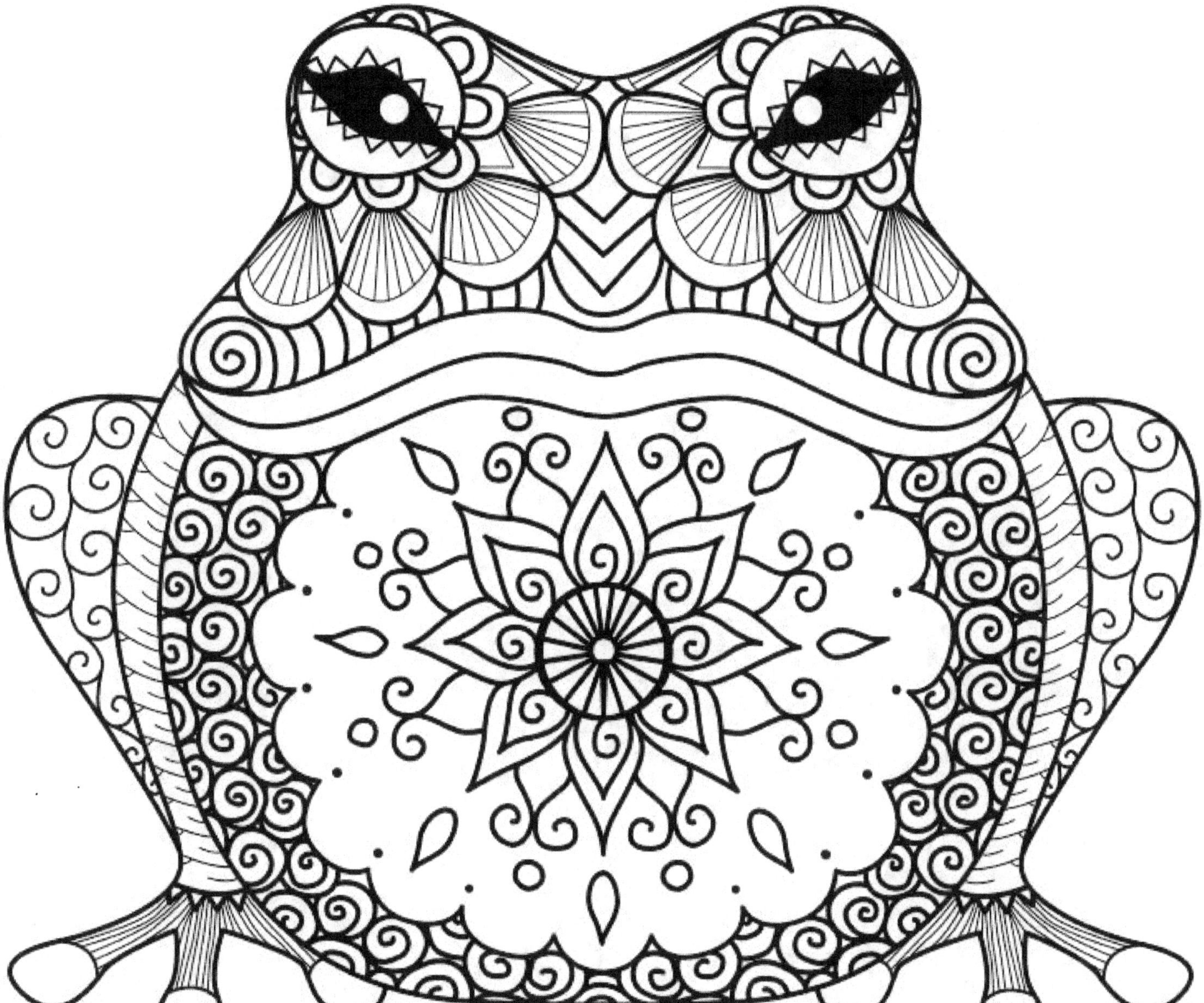

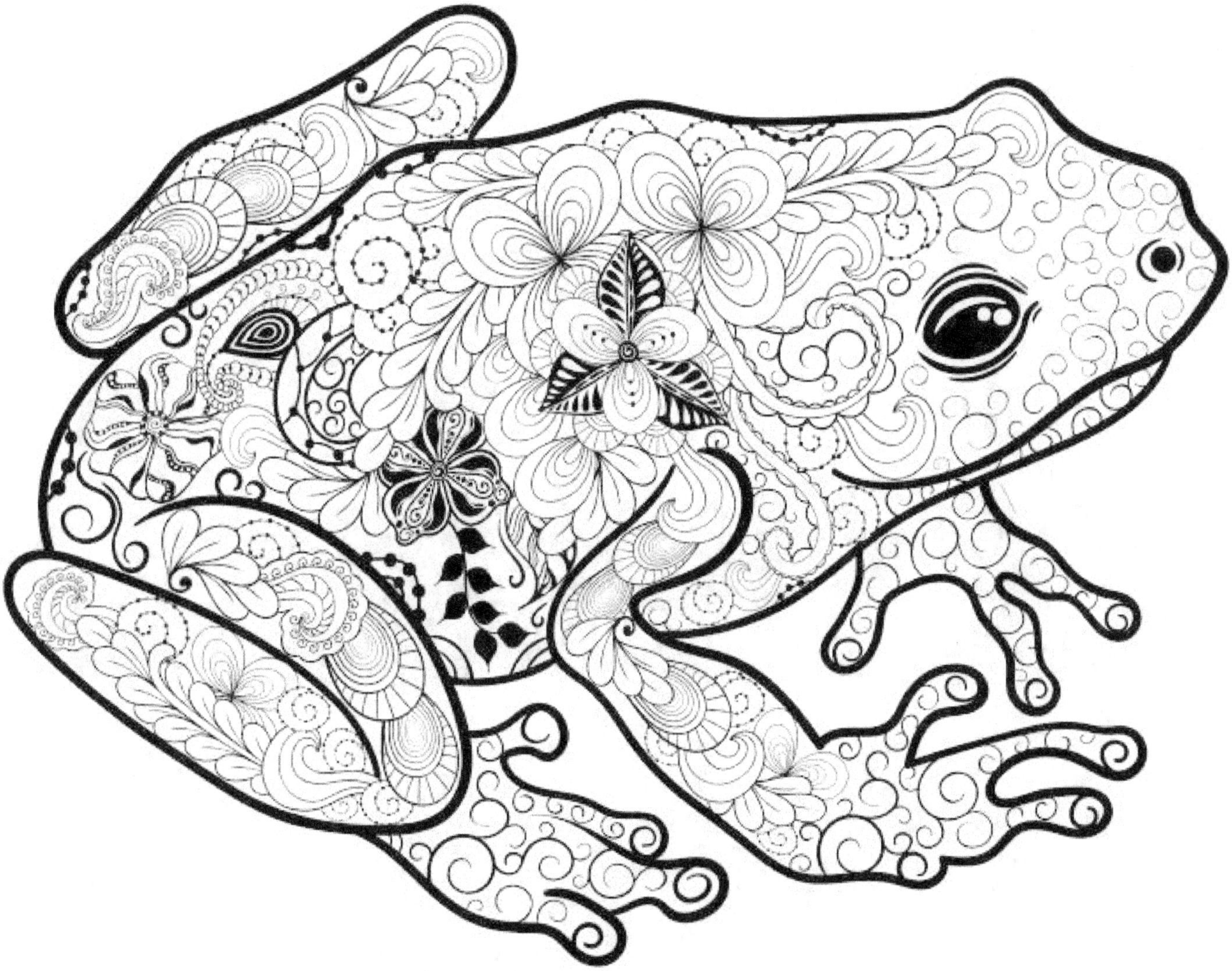

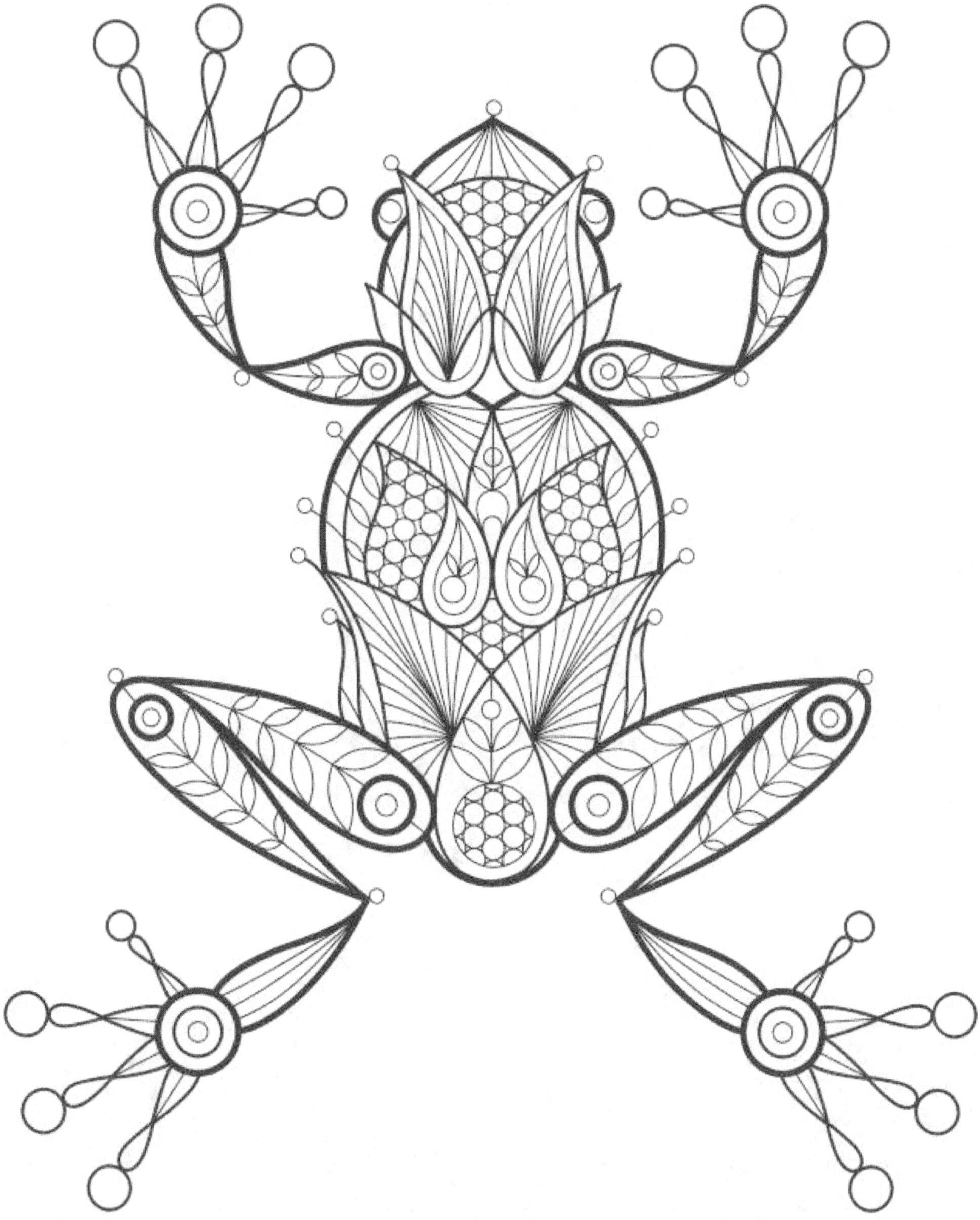

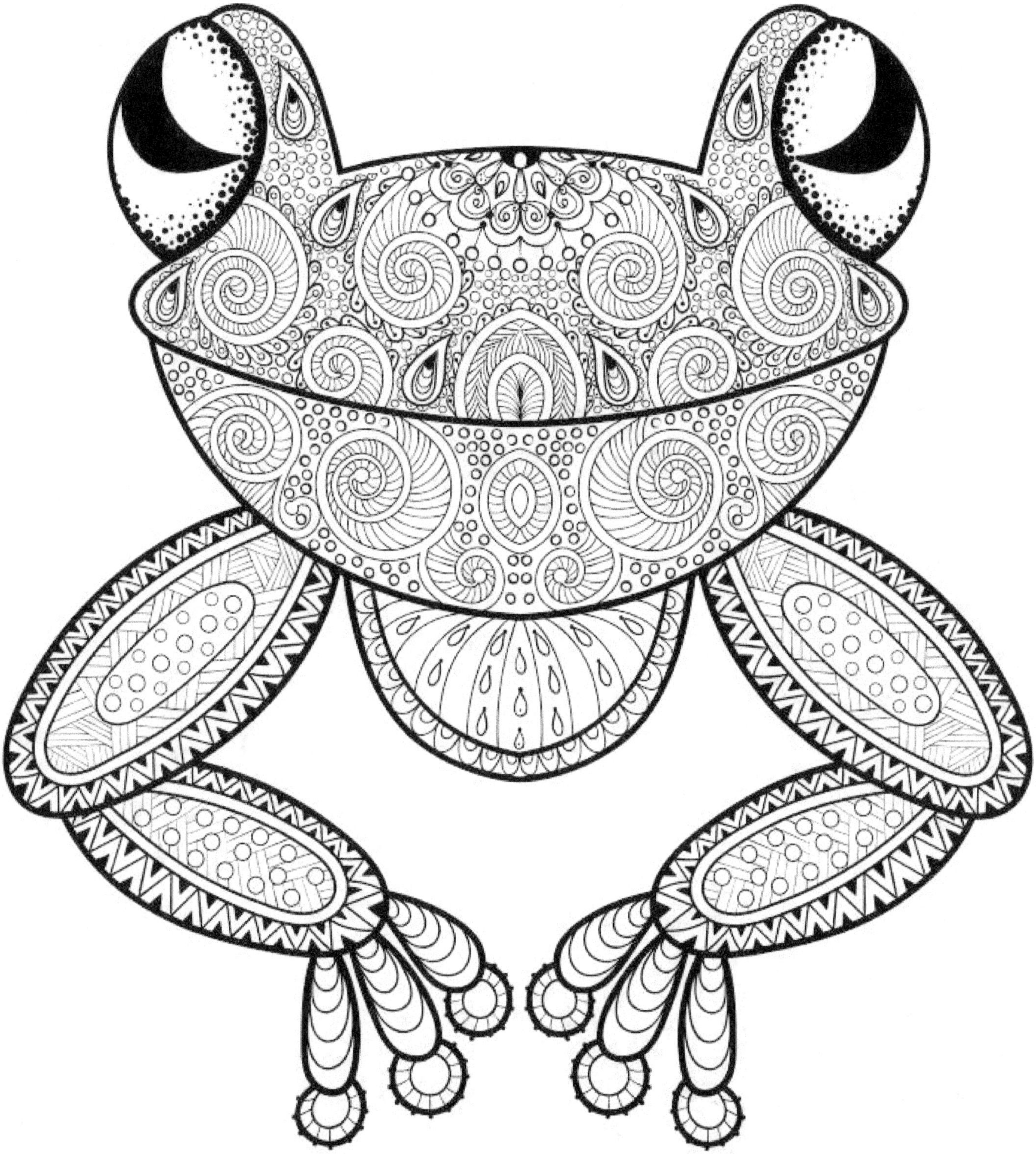

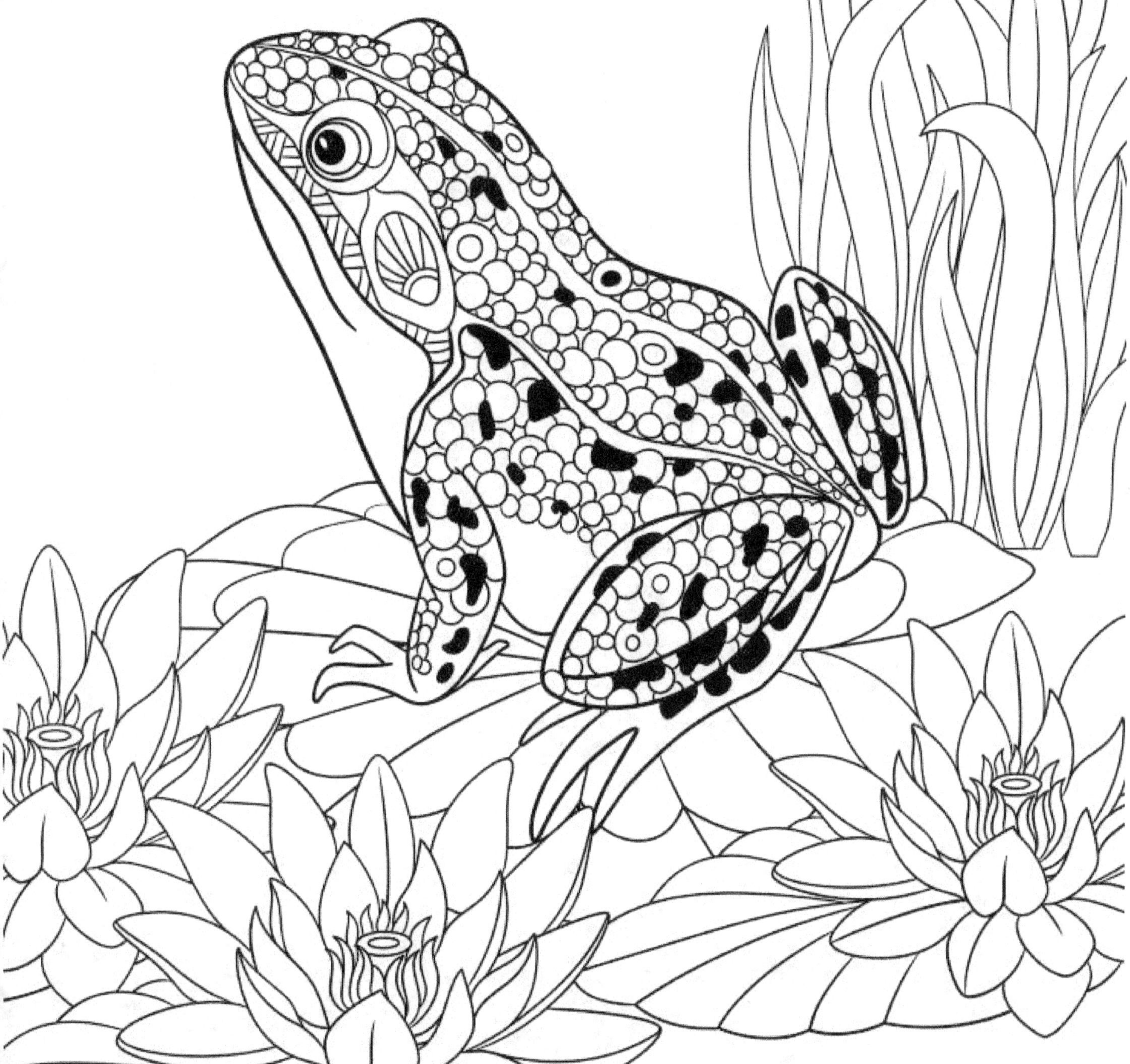

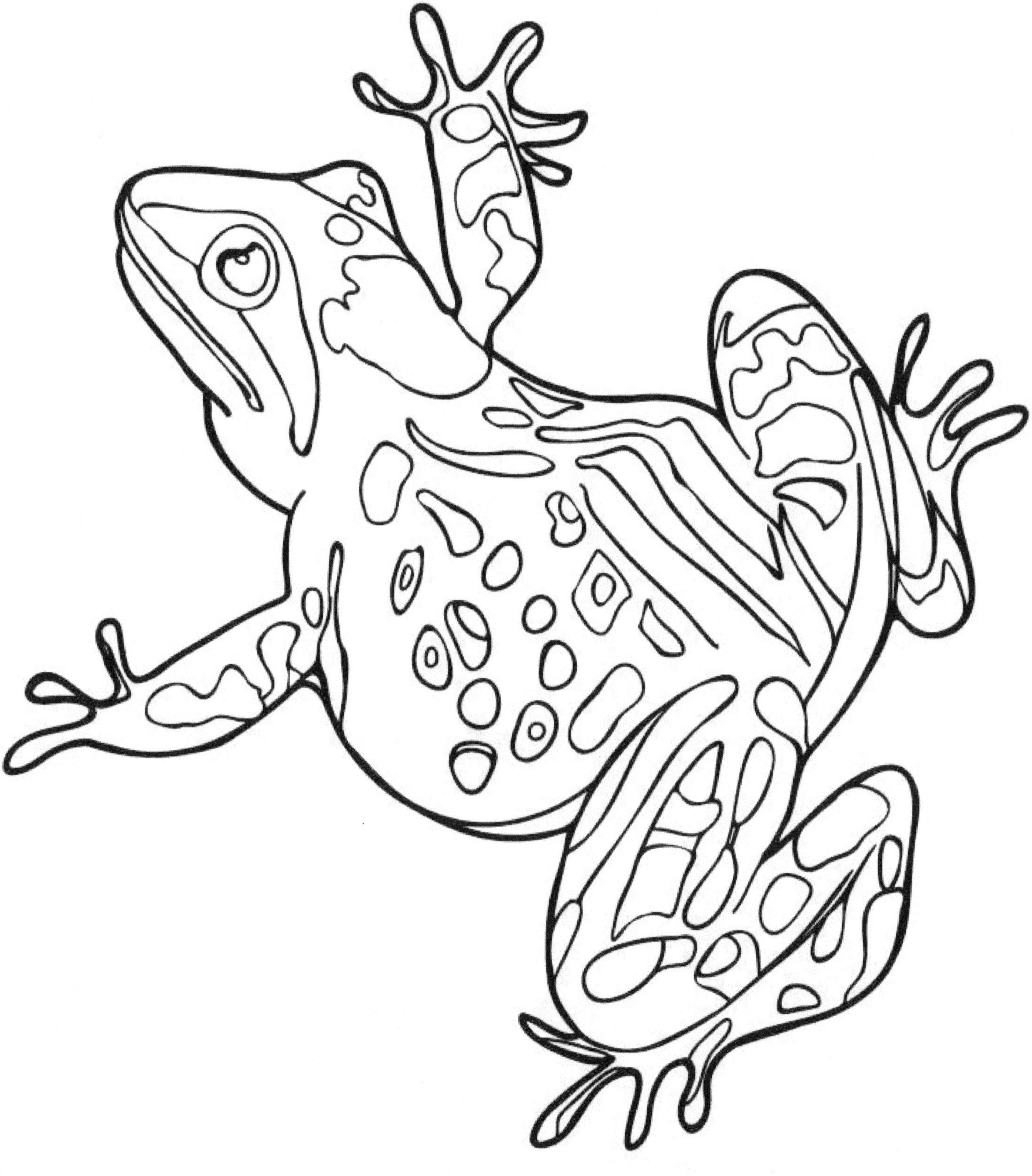

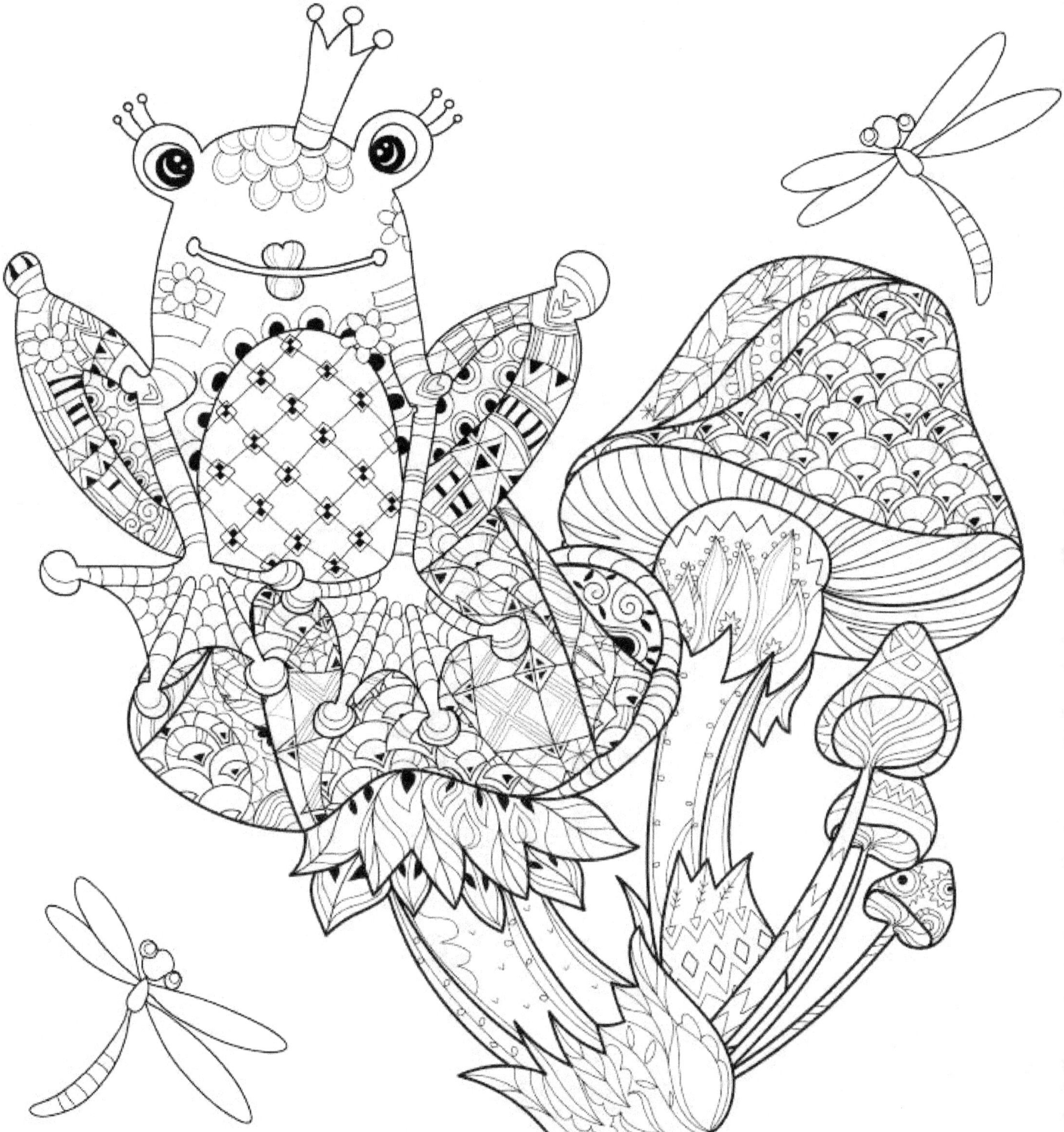

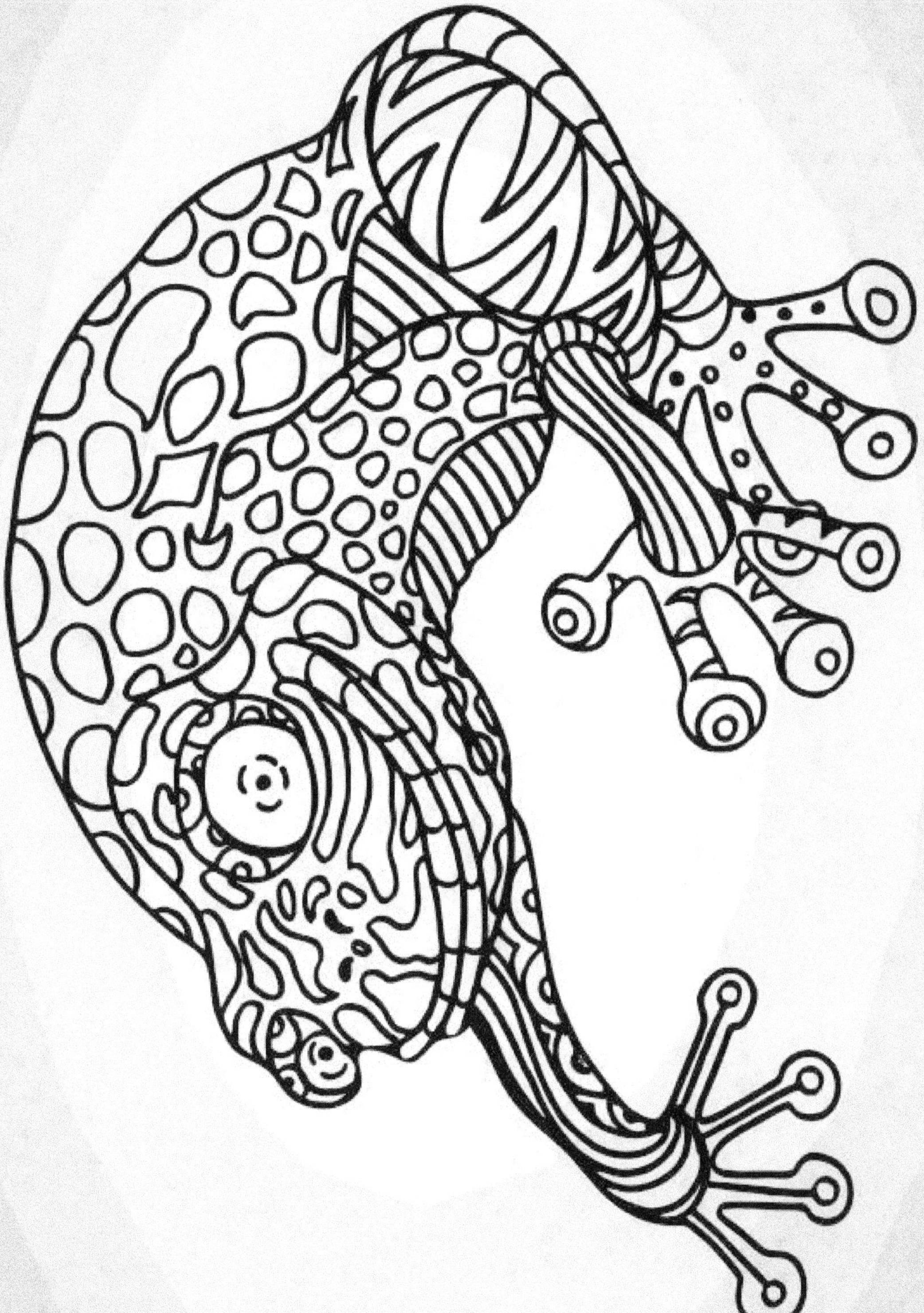

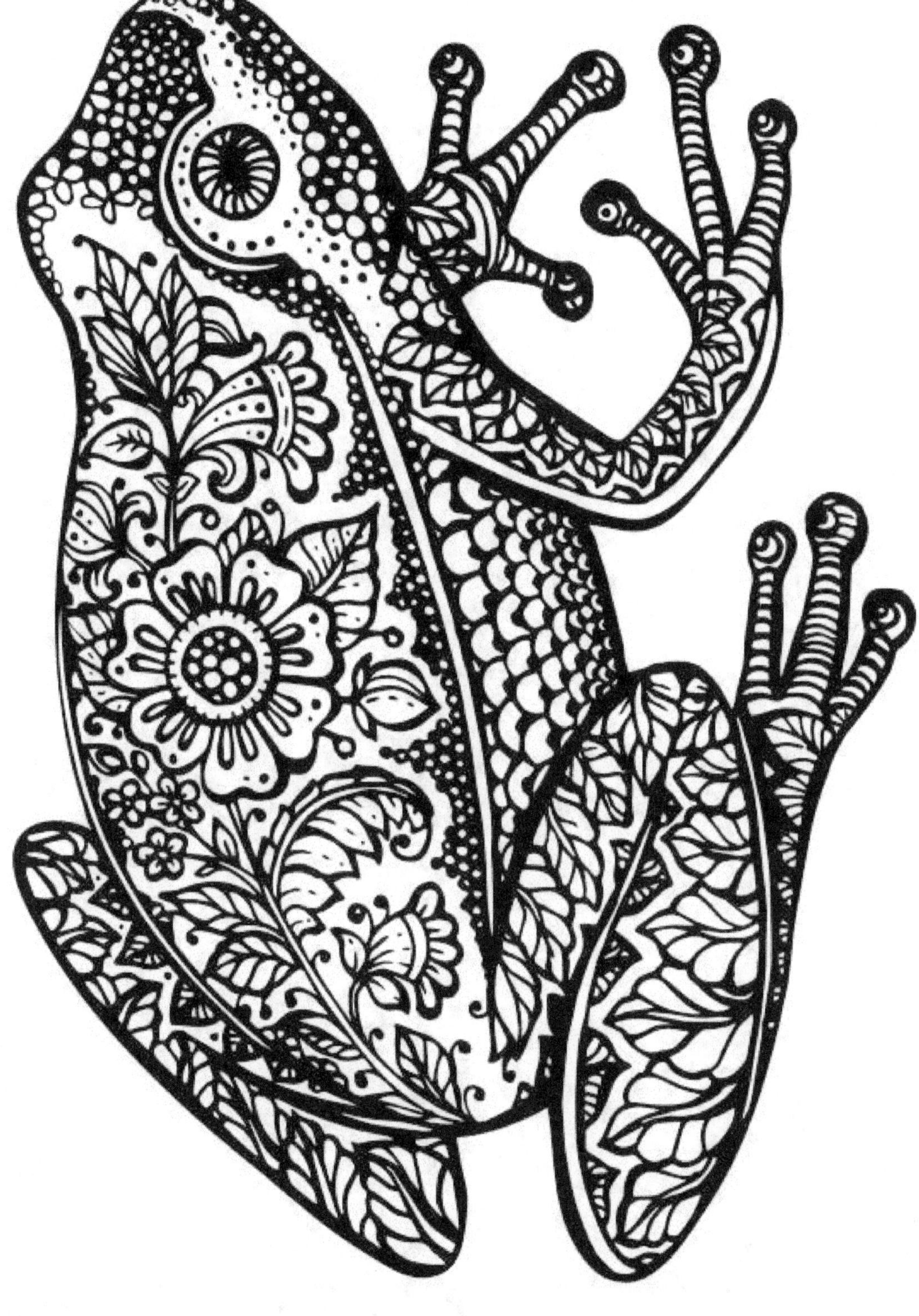

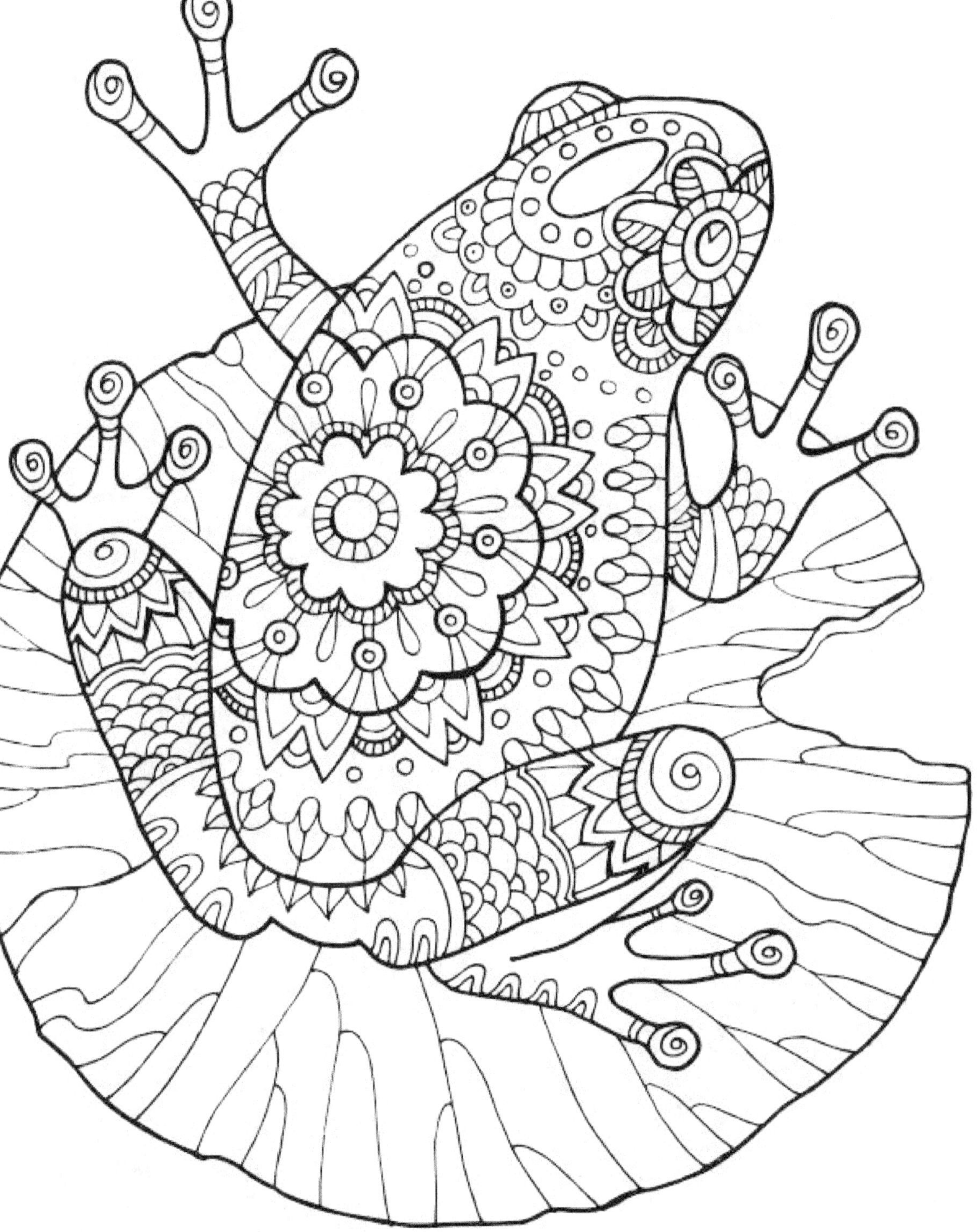

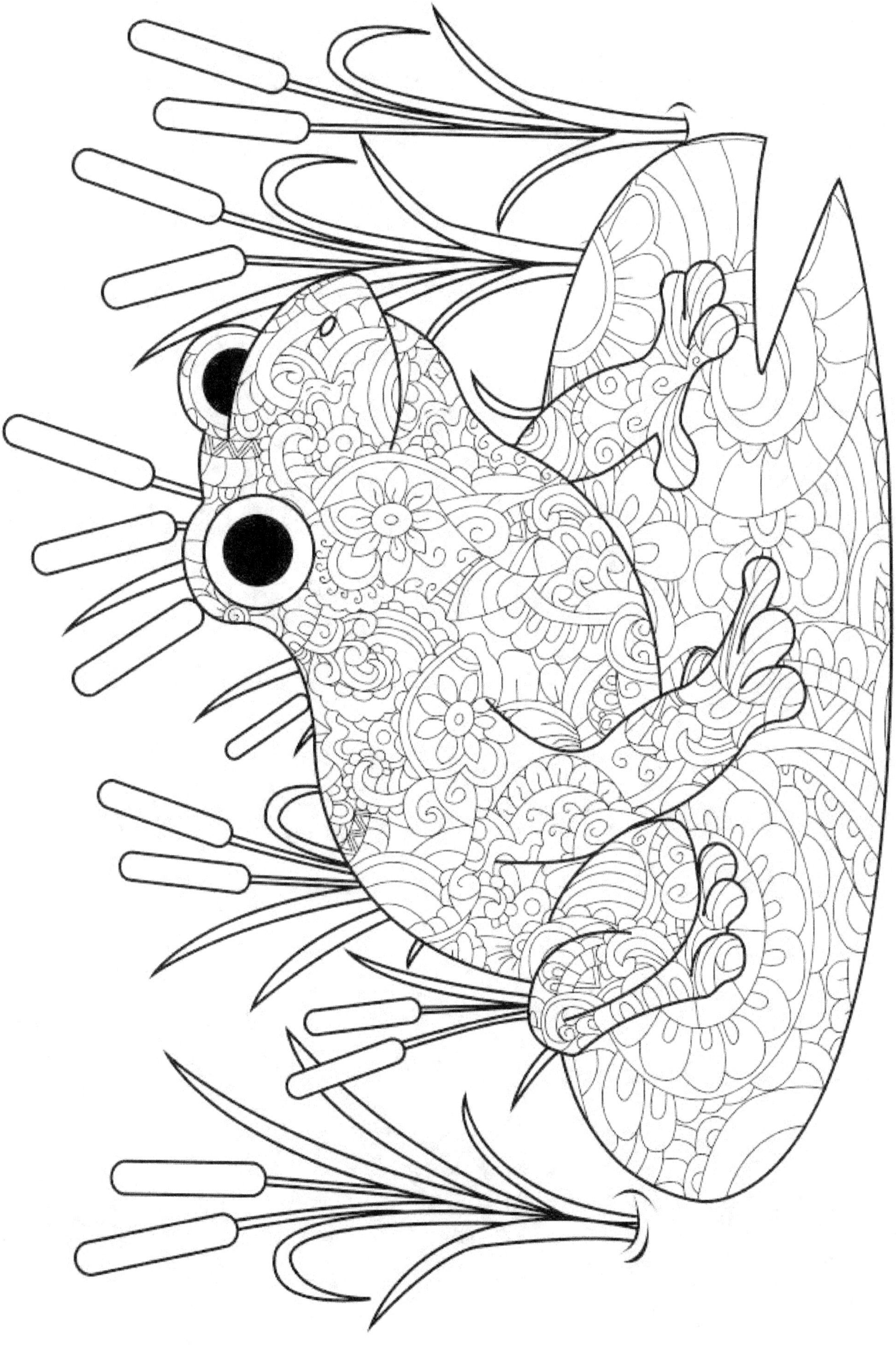

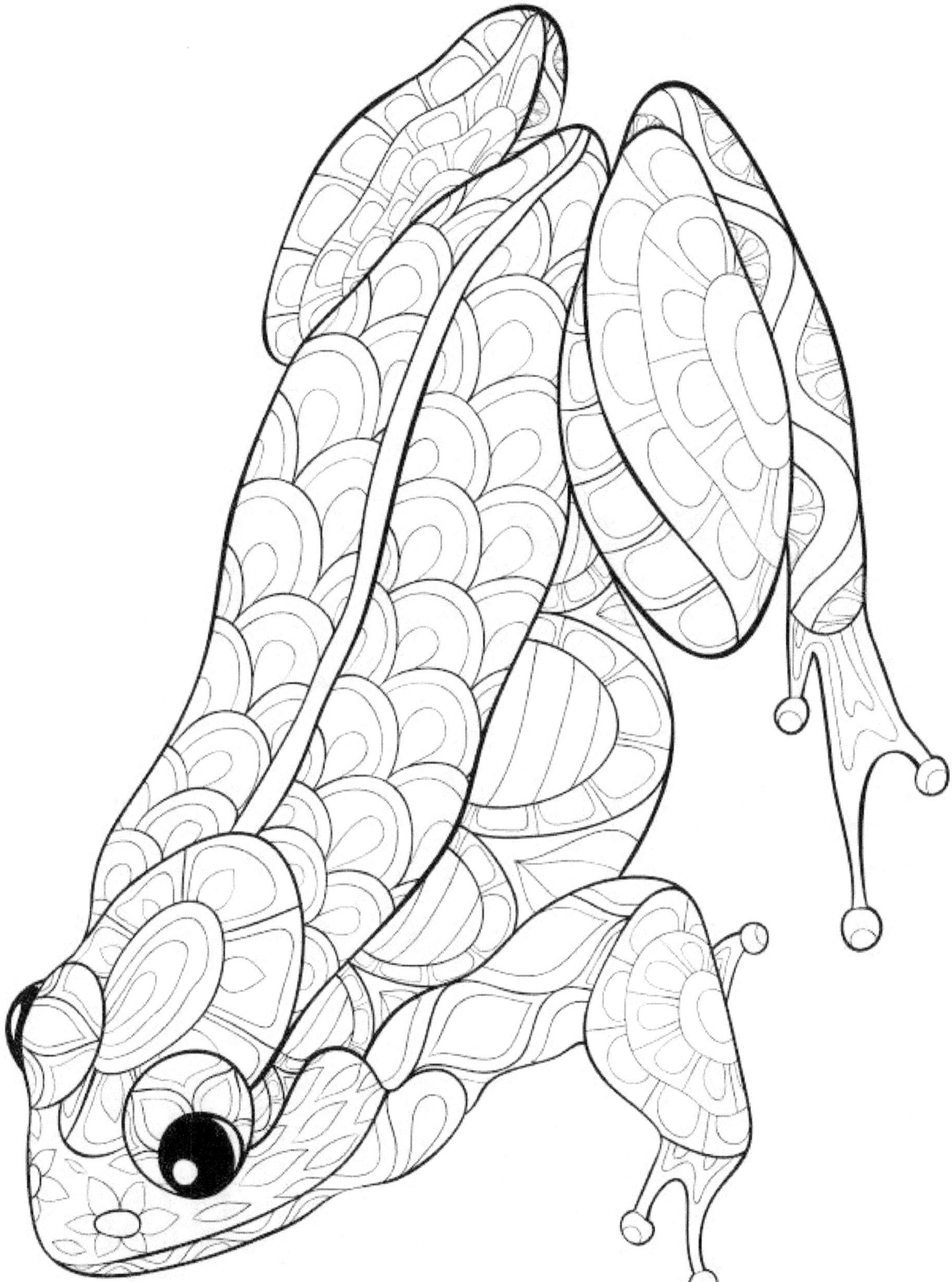

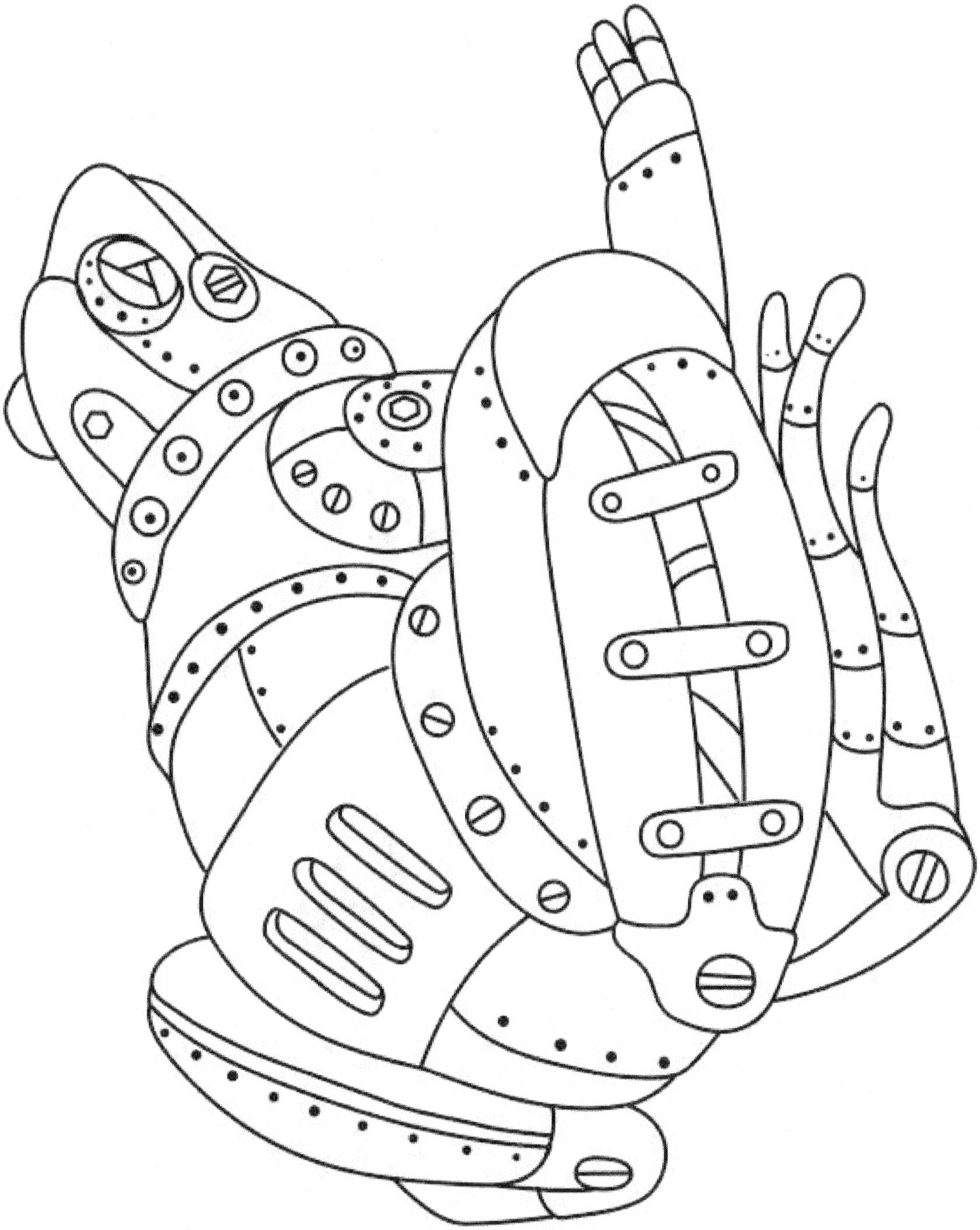

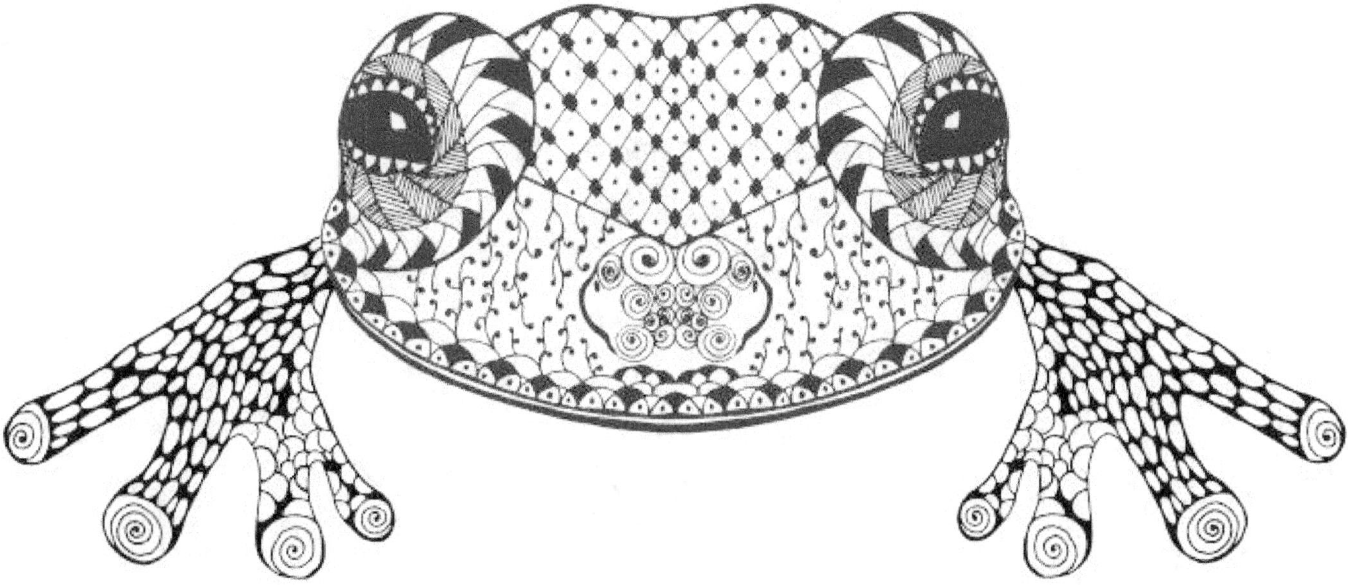

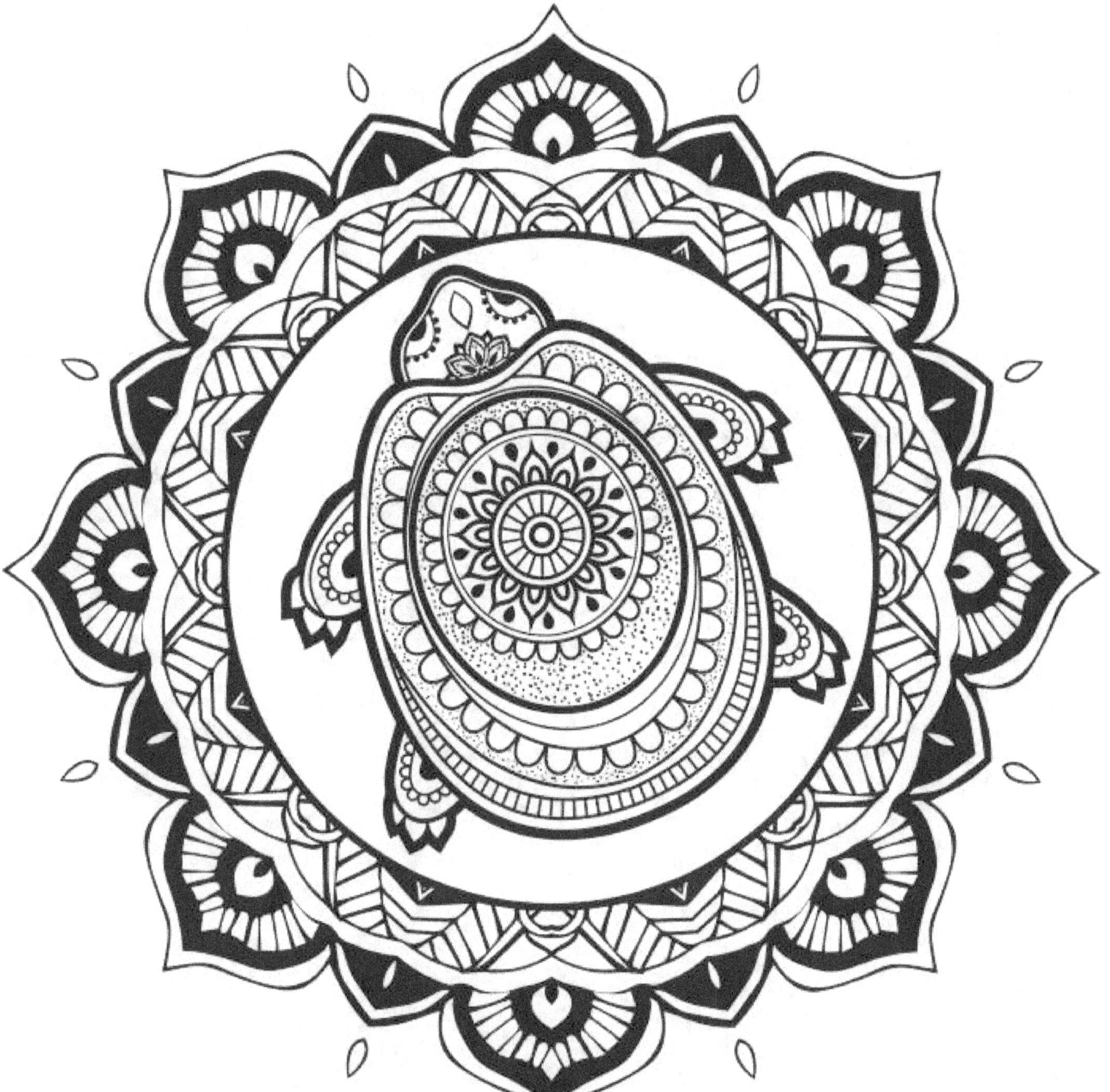

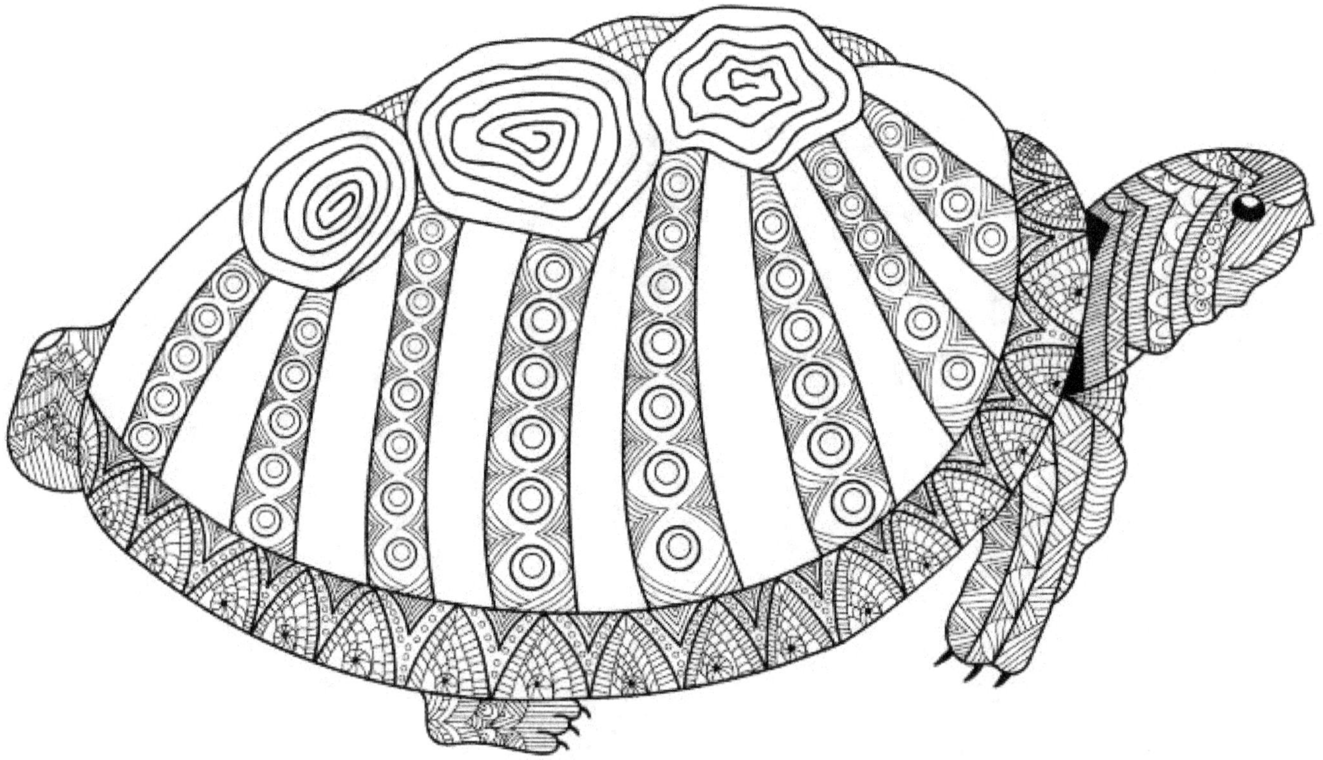

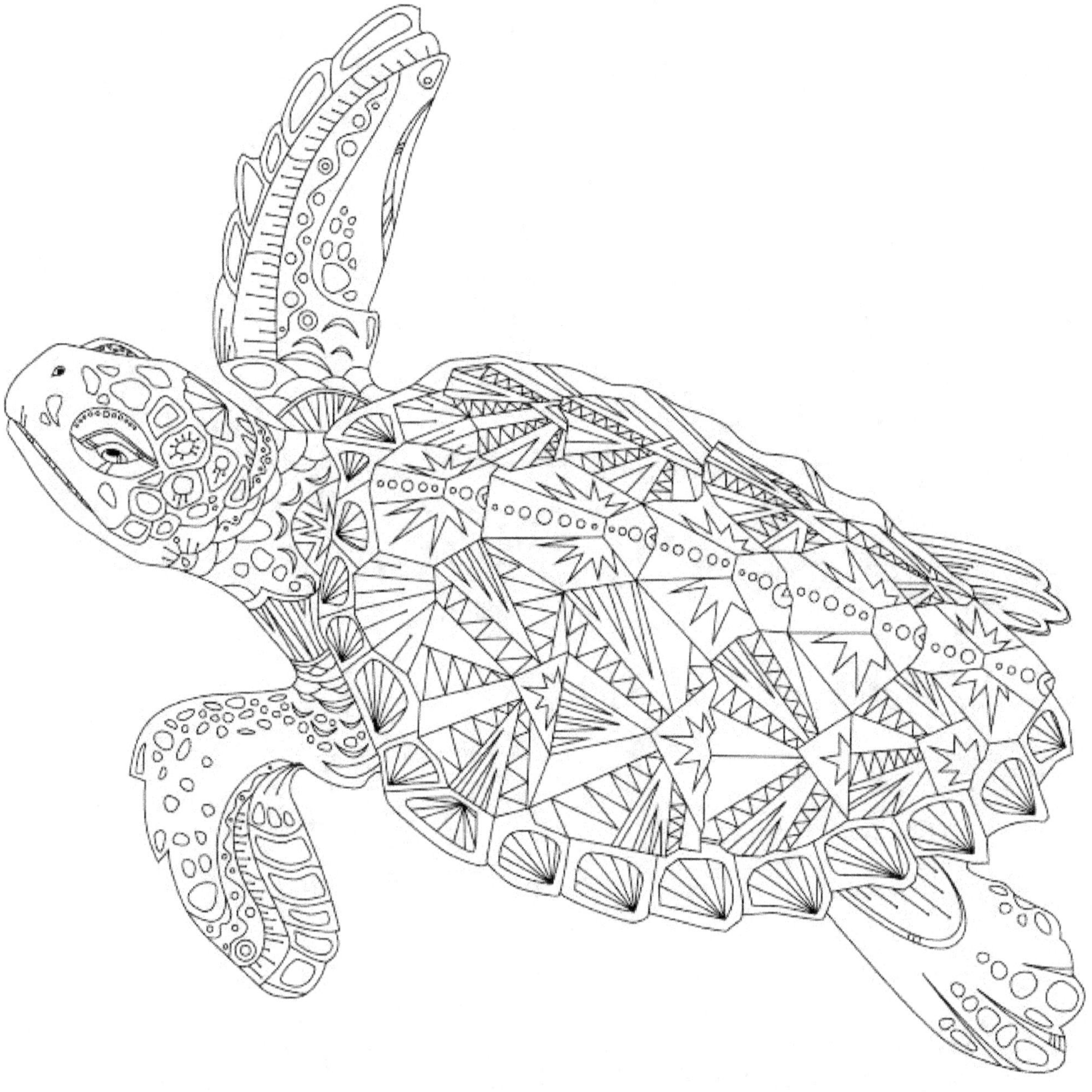

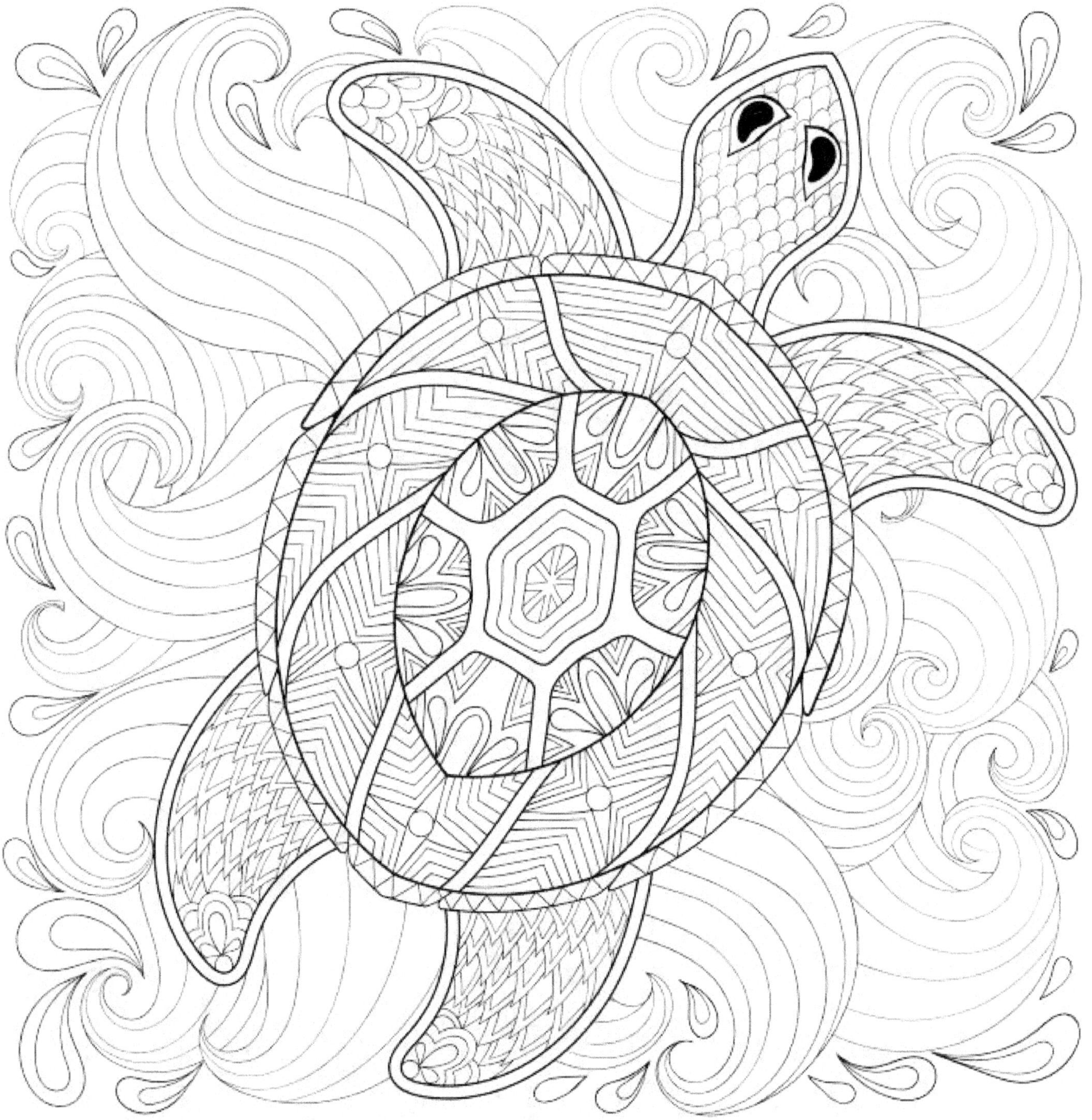

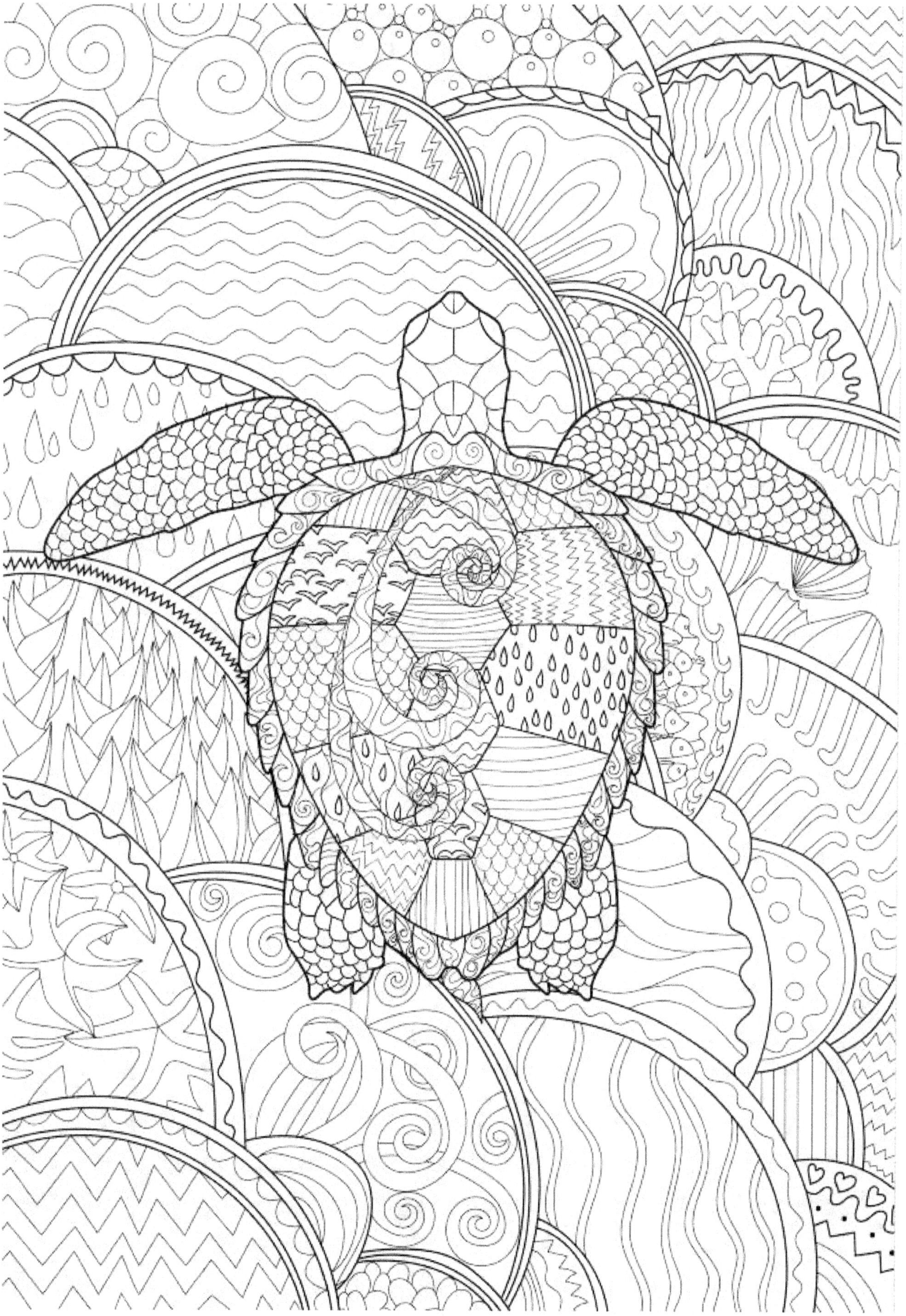

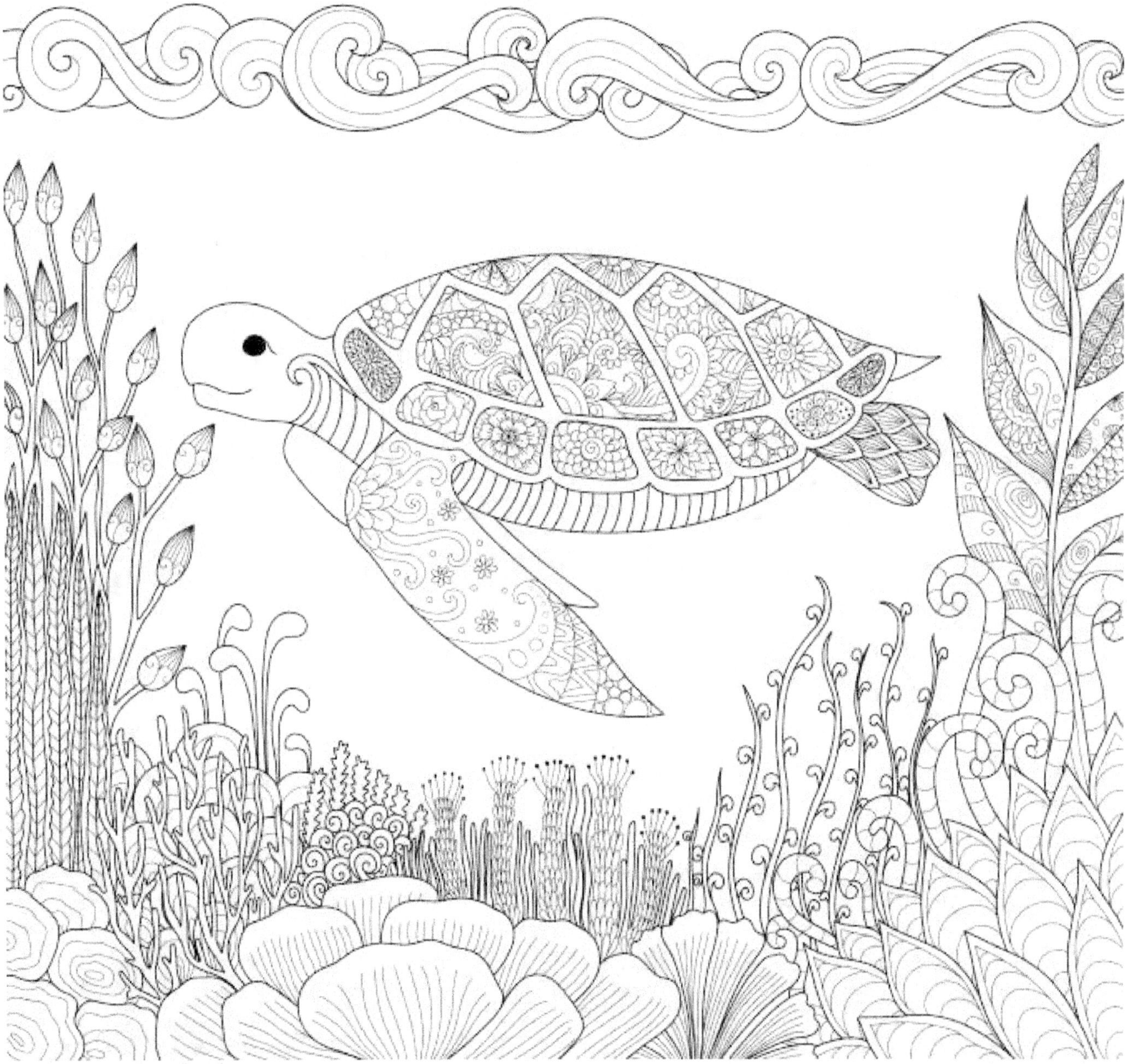

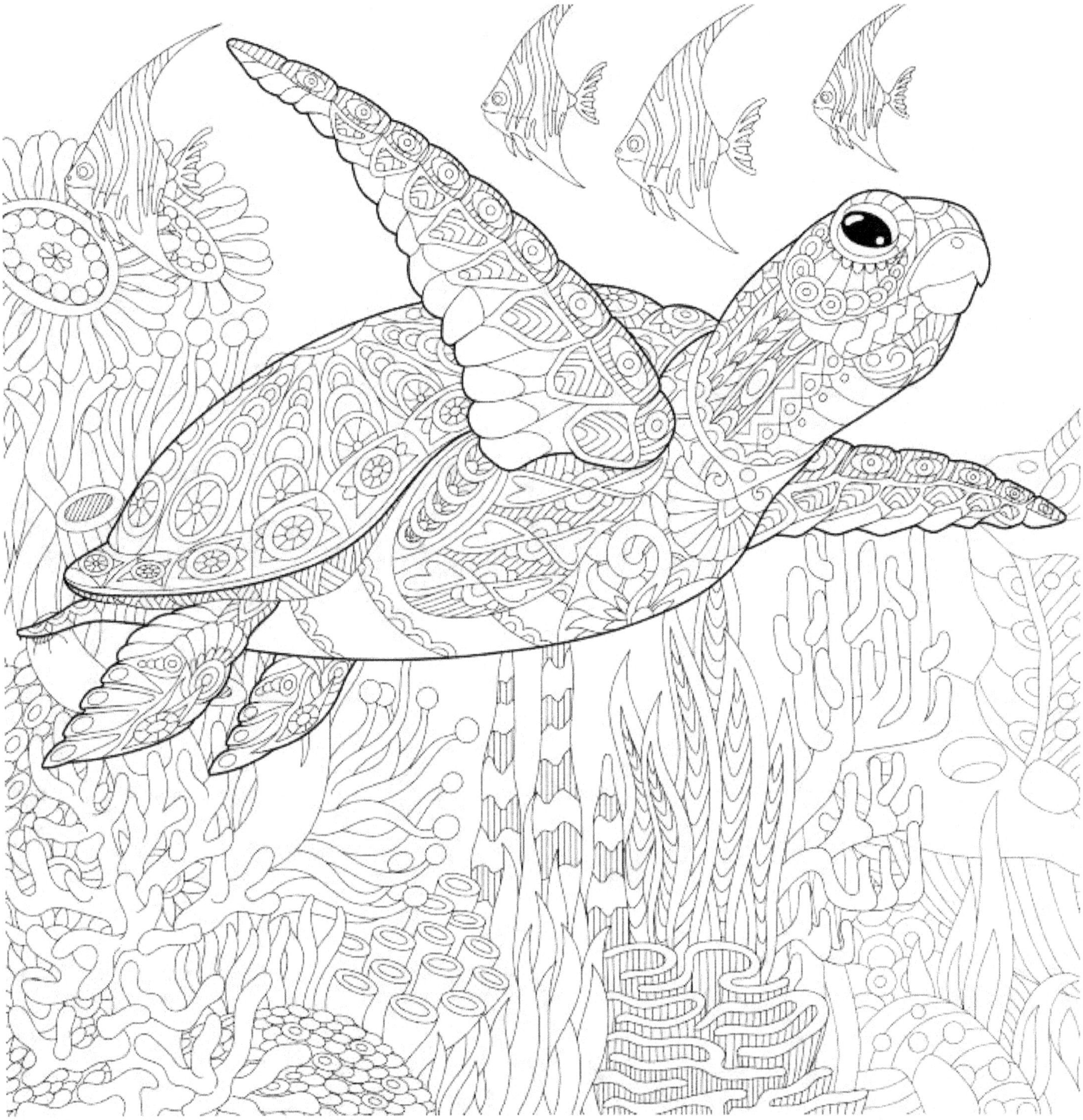

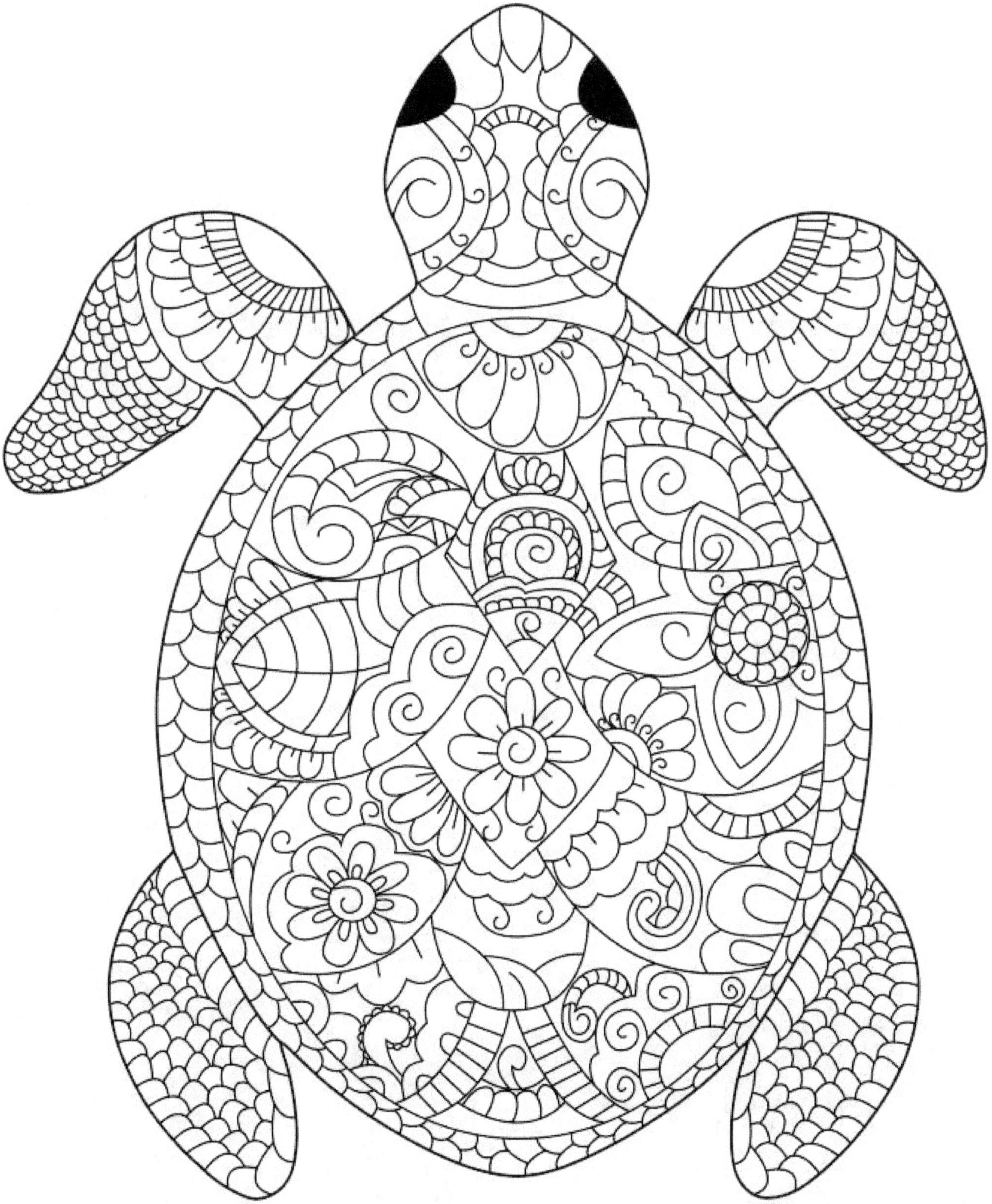

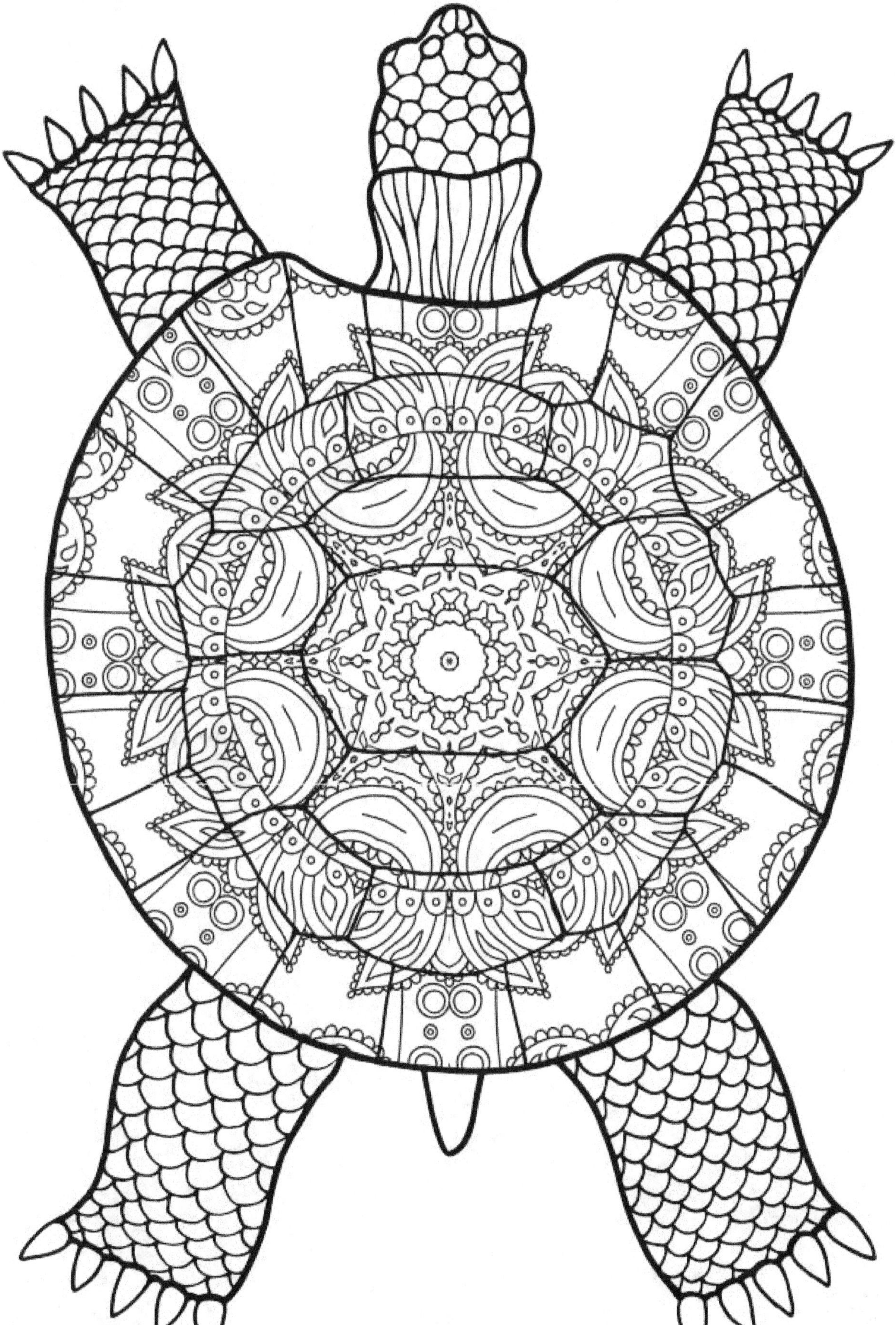

www.ingramcontent.com/pod-product-compliance
Lightning Source LLC
Chambersburg PA
CBHW081300180526
45170CB00007B/2508
9781546943037